W9-CNO-466

Pets at the White House

By Marge Kennedy

Children's Press®
An Imprint of Scholastic Inc.
New York Toronto London Auckland Sydney
Mexico City New Delhi Hong Kong
Danbury, Connecticut

These content vocabulary word builders are for grades 1–2.

Subject Consultant: Eli J. Lesser, MA, Director of Education, National Constitution Center, Philadelphia, Pennsylvania

Reading Consultant: Cecilia Minden-Cupp, PhD, Early Literacy Consultant and Author, Chapel Hill, North Carolina

Photographs © 2009: Alamy Images: 11 (Marvin Dembinsky Photo Associates), 23 bottom right (Larry Lilac); AP Images: cover (Paul Morse/The White House), back cover, 2, 19 (Marcy Nighswander); Corbis Images/Joe McDonald: 5 bottom right, 18; DK Images/Steve Shott: 23 top right; Getty Images: 23 top left (Tony Dawson), 15 (Claudio Edinger), 20 (Stockbyte), 21 all images (GK & Vikki Hart), 7 (Francis Miller/Time Life Pictures), 21 bottom right, 21 top left (Photodisc); ImageState/John Foxx Images: 17; iStockphoto/Mark Hatfield: 13; John Fitzgerald Kennedy Library, Boston: 4 bottom left, 14; Landov, LLC/Roger L. Wollenberg: 1, 4 top, 6; Library of Congress: 5 bottom left, 10 (Harris & Ewing), 5 top right, 5 top left, 8, 16 (Frances Benjamin Johnston Collection), 4 bottom right, 12 (National Photo Company Collection); ShutterStock, Inc.: 23 bottom left (bornholm), 9 (Peter Jilek).

Series Design: Simonsays Design!
Art Direction, Production, and Digital Imaging: Scholastic Classroom Magazines

Library of Congress Cataloging-in-Publication Data

Kennedy, Marge, 1950-
Pets at the White House / Marge Kennedy.
    p. cm. — (Scholastic news nonfiction readers)
Includes bibliographical references and index.
ISBN 13: 978-0-531-21096-3 (lib. bdg.)   978-0-531-22433-5 (pbk.)
ISBN 10: 0-531-21096-0 (lib. bdg.)   0-531-22433-3 (pbk.)
    1. Presidents—United States—Pets—Juvenile literature. 2. Presidents—United States—Biography—Anecdotes—Juvenile literature. 3. Pets—United States—Anecdotes—Juvenile literature. 4. White House (Washington, D.C.)—Juvenile literature. 5. Washington (D.C.)—Social life and customs—Juvenile literature. I. Title.
E176.48.K46 2009
975.3—dc22   2008037429

©2009 Scholastic Inc.
All rights reserved. Published in 2009 by Children's Press, an imprint of Scholastic Inc.
Published simultaneously in Canada. Printed in the United States of America.   44

CONTENTS

WORD HUNT

Look for these words as you read. They will be in **bold**.

dogs
(dawgz)

pony
(**poh**-nee)

raccoon
(ra-**koon**)

4

goat
(goht)

macaw
(muh-**kaw**)

sheep
(sheep)

snake
(snayk)

A House for Pets

Forty-three Presidents have lived in the White House. But more than 100 **dogs** have lived there!

When a President moves into the White House, the President's pets come too.

dogs

These beagles belonged to President Lyndon Johnson.

Do you think a **goat** makes a good pet? Some Presidents thought so.

The grandson of President Benjamin Harrison had a goat named "His Whiskers." The goat pulled the boy in a cart.

goat

Five Presidents have kept goats as pets at the White House.

President Wilson kept **sheep** at the White House. These sheep had a job. They cut the grass! They kept the grass short by eating it.

sheep

A **raccoon** once lived at the White House. Her name was Rebecca. She belonged to President Coolidge. The President's wife liked to walk the raccoon on a leash.

raccoon

Rebecca the raccoon looked a lot like this.

If you lived at the White House, maybe you would have a **pony**!

President Kennedy's children had three ponies. One was called Macaroni.

pony

Caroline Kennedy sat on Macaroni in a family photo.

Theodore Roosevelt's six children had the most pets. They had more than 40!

Young Teddy had a **macaw**. A macaw is a kind of bird. Teddy's sister Alice liked to scare people with her pet. Can you guess what it was?

macaw

Teddy Roosevelt Jr. had a blue macaw like this one. Its name was Eli Yale.

It was a **snake**! Alice's snake was green. She named it Emily Spinach.

If you lived in the White House, what pets would *you* bring?

snake

President Clinton brought his cat, Socks, when he moved into the White House.

HOW MANY RABBITS? HOW MANY PARROTS?

Many kinds of pets have lived at the White House. Some have been more popular than others.

- **What kind of pet has been the most popular?**
- **Have there been more rabbits, or more parrots?**
- **How many more goats than rabbits lived there?**

3 rabbits have lived in the White House.

20 cats have lived in the White House.

7 parrots have lived in the White House.

7 goats have lived at the White House.

111 dogs have lived at the White House.

YOUR NEW WORDS

dogs (dawgz) animals with four legs that are often kept as pets or work animals

goat (goht) an animal with horns and a beard that is sometimes raised for its milk

macaw (muh-**kaw**) a tropical bird with brightly colored feathers

pony (**poh**-nee) a kind of horse that stays small even when fully grown

raccoon (ra-**koon**) an animal with black-and-white face markings that look like a mask

sheep (sheep) a farm animal that is raised for milk, wool, and meat

snake (snayk) a long, thin animal with no legs that moves along the ground

MORE PETS AT THE WHITE HOUSE

Thomas Jefferson was given bears.

Franklin Pierce had two tiny dogs like this.

Abraham Lincoln's son had a turkey.

Ronald Reagan had a goldfish.

23

INDEX

FIND OUT MORE

Book:
Davis, Gibbs. *Wackiest White House Pets*. New York:
Scholastic Press, 2004.

Website:
Presidential Pet Museum
www.presidentialpetmuseum.com

MEET THE AUTHOR
Marge Kennedy's cat, Max, would love to get his claws into
that plush White House furniture.